101 A

© 2018 101 Amazing Things

All rights reserved. No part of this publication may be reproduced, distributed, or transmitted in any form or by any means, including photocopying, recording, or other electronic or mechanical methods, without the prior written permission of the publisher, except in the case of brief quotations embodied in critical reviews and certain other noncommercial uses permitted by copyright law.

Introduction

So you're going to Bali, huh? You are very very lucky indeed! You are sure in for a treat because Bali is, without a doubt, one of the most special travel destinations on the face of the earth. It offers something for every visitor, so whether you are into exploring the spicy Balinese food, unforgettable adventures in the water, or celebrating with locals at music festivals, Bali has something for you.

In this guide, we'll be giving you the low down on:
- the very best things to shove in your pie hole, whether you want to chow down on the Balinese version of meatballs, or you feel like indulging at a chocolate factory
- incredible festivals, from local religious festivals at the many Hindu temples dotted around the island, or epic electronic music festivals on the beach
- the coolest historical and cultural sights that you simply cannot afford to miss like 10th century Hindu temples and contemporary Balinese art galleries
- the most incredible outdoor adventures, whether you want to swim with tropical fish in the ocean or you'd like to get your heart racing by climbing an active volcano

- where to shop for authentic souvenirs so that you can remember your trip to Bali forever
- the places where you can party like a local and make new friends
- and tonnes more coolness besides!

Let's not waste any more time – here are the 101 most amazing, spectacular, and cool things not to miss in Bali!

1. Visit One of Bali's Most Important Temples, Tanah Lot

Tanah Lot is a little bit removed from the main tourist drag of Bali, but it's well worth visiting, particularly if you are interested in the cultural and historic aspects of the island. Located in Kediri, this is one of the seven sea temples in Bali, acting as a protector of bad vibes that might lap up on the shore. We don't know the exact history of the temple, but it was allegedly created in the 16th century. A number of sea caves have formed at the bottom of the temple, which is home to sea snakes said to protect the temple from evil spirits.

(www.tanahlot.net/home)

2. Eat the Best Ice Cream of Your Life at Gusto Gelato & Caffe

Bali is swelteringly hot right throughout the year, and what better way is there to cool down than by chomping on creamy ice cold ice cream? There are many spots to buy ice cream in Bali, but the very best has to be Gusto Gelato & Caffe, which you'll find in the Badung area, a little out of the way. They only use fresh ingredients, and you can really taste that. There are many exotic flavours to choose from, such as turmeric, soursop, and avocado-chocolate. *(Jl. Mertanadi No.46B, Kerobokan Kelod, Kuta Utara, Kabupaten Badung; http://gusto-gelateria.com)*

3. Take in the Drama of the Kecak Fire Dances

The Uluwatu Temple, one of the important sea temples that you can find located on the coast of Bali, is well worth visiting, but be sure to get there in the evening time. First of all, because it's one of the best places to watch the sunset. But also because every day at 6pm, you have the opportunity to see the Kecak Fire Dances in action. This is a dance show that also involves chanting, and is based on the Hindu story of the Ramayana.

4. Take Surfing Lessons at Suluban Beach

Whether you are a newbie to surfing or you regularly ride the waves, Bali is an absolute paradise for surfers of all abilities, and you shouldn't miss the opportunity to improve your surfing ability while there. There are so many beaches with great surfing, but our top pick is Suluban Beach, which has massive waves from 3 to 12 feet, but doesn't have the crowds of some of the neighbouring party beaches. You'll have no problems finding surfboard rentals or surf lessons.

5. Tuck Into a Huge Place of Nasi Goreng

Nasi Goreng isn't specifically a Balinese dish because it is popular right across Indonesia, but we think that it's such a staple dish that you'll be chowing down on plenty of it during your visit to Bali. This dish consists of fried rice mixed with flavourings such as shrimp paste, tamarind, chilli, shallots, and garlic. There will typically be some protein such as chicken, egg, or prawns mixed in too. It's cheap, filling, and incredibly tasty.

6. Indulge a History Buff at Gunung Kawi

While Bali is mostly thought of as a beach and party destination, it is also very rich culturally, and something that culture and history buffs shouldn't miss is the Gunung Kawi temple, located a little north of Ubud. This 11th century temple consists of 11 ancient candi, which can be thought of as shrines, which stand majestically at a height of 8 metres, cut directly into niches in a cliff face.

Each of the candi is said to represent a member of 11th century Balinese royalty, but we can't know this for sure. *(Banjar Penaka, Tampaksiring, Kabupaten Gianyar)*

7. Try the Local Street Food, Nasi Jinggo

When you are ready for something tasty to eat but you want to avoid another experience jostling with tourists in a restaurant, or you simply want to save some money, street food is the way to go. One of our favourite street bites, which can really be a full meal, is called Nasi Jinggo. This is a banana leaf that contains all kinds of surprises inside: a mix of steamed rice and noodles, shredded coconut, shredded chicken, and spicy sambal.

8. Have an Artsy Day at Neka Art Museum

If you're an arts lover, you might be more inclined to visit Paris or Florence than Bali, but actually there is more of an arts culture on the island than you might imagine, and the Neka Art Museum is a place you should definitely try and check out. This private gallery is dedicated to Balinese painting, but it's far from one note as the local styles vary

hugely. There is a permanent exhibit, rotating temporary exhibits, a bookshop, and even a café on the premises.
(Jalan Raya Sanggingan Campuhan, Kedewatan, Ubud, Kabupaten Gianyar; www.museumneka.com)

9. Take in a Drag Show at the Bali Beach Shack

Looking for some cool entertainment during your stay in Bali? Then you should look no further than the Bali Beach Shack, a cool beach bar and restaurant on Legian beach with one of the best views, but that's not the reason we go there. The reason the punters keep going back to the Bali Beach Shack is because of the incredible nightly drag shows. The performers are energetic and put on one hell of a show, and the whole thing is family friendly.
(Jl. Sahadewa No.7, Legian, Kuta; http://balibeachshack.com)

10. Surround Yourself With Butterflies at Bali Butterfly Park

When you can't take another beach party and you just want to immerse yourself in the beauty of local nature, one of the best spots to recuperate and take in the gorgeousness of Bali is the Bali Butterfly Park in remote

Wansari village. This park is said to be the largest of its kind anywhere in Asia, and it has hundreds upon hundreds of butterfly species that fly all around you. If you have kids, this is a great half day family trip too.

(Jl. Batukaru, Sandan Lebah, Sesandan, Buruan, Penebel, Kabupaten Tabanan; www.balitravelhub.com/attractions/bali-butterfly-park)

11. Hike Through the Sangeh Monkey Forest

On a tropical island like Bali, it can be all too easy to kick back on a sun lounger day after day while sipping on cocktails. While there's nothing wrong with that, if you're a more active person, there are plenty of gorgeous hikes you can do on the island. One of our favourite spots to strap on the walking boots is the Sangeh Monkey Forest. There's huge nutmeg trees and lots of space for ambling around, and as the name of the forest would suggest, lots of monkeys too. They are attracted to shiny things, so maybe hide your jewellery.

(Jl. Brahmana, Sangeh, Abiansemal, Kabupaten Badung; http://bukit-sari-sangeh.com)

12. Eat a Local Breakfast of Nasi Tepeng in Gianyar

Although Bali is a relatively small island in its own right, you'll be amazed by the diversity of the cuisine there, and how it can change from town to town. Something you will only find in the Gianyar part of the island is a yummy breakfast dish that goes by the name of Nasi Tepeng. This is a rice dish but the texture is somewhat mushy, approaching porridge. The rice is topped with shredded chicken, egg, jackfruit, beans, and aubergine.

13. Sleep Above a Shrimp Pond at the Bambu Indah Hotel

There are accommodations to suit every budget and every style of travel in Bali, but what if you want something that's a little out of the ordinary and is not just somewhere to rest your head, but part of your Bali experience? Then we would wholeheartedly recommend the Bambu Indah Hotel in Ubud. For a start, the whole thing is made from bamboo and is totally gorgeous. But what really makes it stand out is the shrimp pong beneath some of the rooms. The rooms have a glass floor so you are literally walking on water and seeing the shrimp swim around beneath you. *(Jl. Banjar Baung, Desa, Sayan, Ubud; http://bambuindah.com)*

14. Hike to the Gorgeous Sekumpul Waterfall

For us, there is nothing quite as relaxing as standing in front of a gushing waterfall, and feeling perfectly at one with nature. There are lots of waterfalls around Bali, and Sekumpul Waterfall is one of the most impressive. Located in remote Sekumpul village, it's a lovely trek to get there, during which you'll be surrounded by towering durian and rambutan trees. When you arrive, you'll be greeted by not one, not two, but seven waterfalls. It's well worth the effort of getting off the main tourist trail to see it.

15. Take in the View of the Tegallalang Rice Terraces

We think that one of the most beautifully serene views that you can ever experience is a vista of green rice paddies. Fortunately, Bali is a rice growing island so there are a few places where you can see the rice paddies, but the most breath taking of them all would have to be the Tegallalang Rice Terraces. If you want to relax and take in the view, there are cafes at the top, but you can also hike into and up the rice paddies, which is well worth doing if you have some energy. It takes about an hour.

(Jalan Tegallalang, Tegallalang, Kabupaten Gianyar)

16. Check Out Balinese Masks in Ubud

Bali is not just a beach island but a very cultural place, and a unique part of the local culture are the masks that are created and worn for festivals and ceremonies. A place where you can see these is a fantastic museum in Ubud that goes by the name of the Setia Darma House of Masks & Puppets. Inside you'll find more than 7000 masks and puppets from Bali and other places in Indonesia, displayed in a set of incredible renovated historic buildings.

(Jalan Tegal Bingin, Mas, Ubud; http://setiadarmabali.com)

17. Look to the Skies During the Bali Kite Festival Sanur

The annual Bali Kite Festival in Sanur is serious business. We're not talking a few local people running across the beach with their kites, but over 1000 competitors from all over the world showing what they've got to 10,000 spectators. As you can probably imagine, the amount of colour in the sky is simply breath taking, and the atmosphere is buzzing with excitement. It happens across a weekend in mid-July each year, so make sure you are part of it.

18. Tuck Into Roasted Pork at Babi Guling Pak Malen

You might think that on a hot tropical island like Bali, you'd be presented with light salads, but actually the local food can be very hearty and meat heavy. Babi guling is the Balinese version of roast suckling pig, and it's every bit as delicious as it sounds. The best place for it is a very local joint that goes by the name of Babi Guling Pak Malen. The pig is stuffed with deliciousness like turmeric, coriander seeds, black pepper, garlic, and lemongrass. Be sure to get some of the crunchy crackling too.

(Jl. Sunset Road No.554, Seminyak, Kuta; http://babi-guling-pak-malen.business.site)

19. Fill Your Stomach at Gianyar Night Market

One of the best things that you can do in Bali is eat. Because of the popularity of the island there are a lot of eating options, but this also means that food can sometimes be overpriced. The solution is to make your way to Gianyar Night Market, which is remote enough for it not to be overrun by tourists, and to have very local prices. In fact, the portions are so big and the food is so cheap that it's worth taking a group of people to share all of the yumminess.

(Jl. Ngurah Rai, Gianyar, Kec. Gianyar)

20. Say Hi to the Birds at Bali Bird Park

Want to get back to nature and connect with the greenery and wildlife of Bali? Then look no further than the Bali Bird Park, which takes over an area of more than 2000 square metres, and contains over 1000 birds that belong to more than 250 species. If you have kids, you'll be pleased to know that this is a place the whole family can enjoy. There is interactive feeding, Bird of Prey shows, and lots more fun besides.

(Jl. Serma Cok Ngurah Gambir, Singapadu, Batubulan, Sukawati; www.balibirdpark.com)

21. Shop for Beautiful Things at Sukawati Art Market

Bali is more than a destination for surfers and beach bums, and if you want to explore the local arts scene and take some of that art home with you, we'd heartily recommend a trip to the Sukawati Art Market, which comprises 2 stories so there is plenty to enjoy. Furthermore, there is something for every taste and every budget. You can find everything from dramatic oil paintings to handcrafted notebooks, and just about anything artsy in between.

(Jalan Raya Sukawati, Sukawati)

22. Learn About Coffee at the Munduk Moding Coffee Plantation

Are you the kind of person who can't start the day without a strong cup of coffee? You are not alone, but if you want to know the story behind your beloved coffee, a good place to visit is the Mundok Moding Coffee Plantation where you can see the coffee growing in the wild, and learn more about the harvesting process. This coffee plantation also boasts luxury accommodation and a spa, so why not treat yourself?

(Jalan Raya Asah Gobleg, Gobleg;
www.mundukmodingplantation.com)

23. Get Artsy at the Bali Arts Festival Denpasar

Bali is a beach bum's paradise, but it's also a surprisingly artsy place, and the arts culture of Bali really peaks in the summer months for the annual Bali Arts Festival in Denpasar, running across June until mid-July. The festival has a particular focus on the performing arts, and the whole of Denpasar really comes to life during this time. Whether you would like to watch an orchestral performance, shadow puppetry, or contemporary dance, there will be something for you.

24. Enjoy a Lazy Sunday at Sanur Sunday Market

If you find yourself in Bali on a Sunday and with no plans, a place we'd highly recommend visiting is the Sanur Sunday Market. This is not the kind of bustling street market that will leave you more stressed out than relaxed, but a quiet market where local designers are invited to showcase their wares. There are different vendors every week, and you can find everything from hand printed textiles to glassware, ceramics, and more besides.
(Jalan Danau Tamblingan, Sanur)

25. Eat From the Fresh Seafood Warungs in Jimbaran

Of course, one of the best things about finding yourself on a tropical island surrounded by water is the amount of fresh seafood you can eat. And for us, there's no better place to chow down on treats from the sea than in the small coastal town of Jimbaran. This fishing town is full of warungs (which you can think of as local cafes serving up local food at local prices) that specialise in fresh grilled seafood that has been caught that same day. Simple and so delicious.

26. Have a Diving Adventure off the Coast of Tulamben

Tulamben is a small unassuming fishing village on the north-east coast of Bali, but it also happens to be one of the best spots for diving on the whole island. The reason this area is so popular with divers is not because of tropical fish or coral, but because of the discovery of the USS Liberty Shipwreck in the 1980s. But actually, the shipwreck IS covered with coral and fish, and it's one of the easiest wreck dives in the world. There are plenty of schools there that can take you through the dive experience, even if you're a total beginner.

27. Enjoy Complete Indulgence at Thermes Marins Spa

Going on holiday is the time when you really have the opportunity to kick back, relax, and indulge. And what better way is there to treat yourself to a bit of TLC than by heading to a luxury spa in Bali. If that sounds good to you, look no further than the Thermes Marins Spa. There's a multitude of ways to pamper yourself here, from hot stone treatments to vigorous full body massage, through to relaxing in the seawater jet pools or simply lounging in the manicured tropical gardens.

(AYANA Resort and Spa, Bali, Jl Karang Mas Sejahtera, Jimbaran; www.ayana.com/bali/ayana-resort-and-spa/spa)

28. Cook Balinese Food at Hotel Tugu

As you travel around Bali, you are sure to sample an array of mouth-watering dishes, but how much cooler would it be if you actually knew how to cook Balinese food? Well, you will be able to if you book a cooking class at the acclaimed Hotel Tugu. These classes last for half a day so you really do have the time to pick up some skills, and they involve a trip to a local market to pick up ingredients. You'll make things like bumbu, a spicy paste commonly used in Balinese cooking, and dishes like steamed fish in banana leaves and long bean and chicken salad.

(Jl. Pantai Batu Bolong, Pantai Canggu, Canggu; www.tuguhotels.com/hotels/bali)

29. Hit a Few Balls at the New Kuta Golf Course

If your idea of the perfect getaway doesn't involve museums, beach-time, or even fancy restaurants, but just a few rounds of great golf in a picturesque setting, you'll be pleased to know that you have a number of charming golf courses to choose from in Bali. Our top pick is the New Kuta Golf Course. What sets this course apart from the rest is that it's located on a cliff top, giving you the most incredible views. It also hosted the Indonesian Open in 2009, so it's very well respected amongst pro players.

(Jalan Raya Uluwatu,, Kawasan Pecatu Indah Resort Pecatu, Jimbaran; www.newkutagolf.com)

30. Enter a Different World at the 3D Dream Museum Zone

The 3D Dream Museum Zone is one of the more left-of-centre attractions to be found in Bali, but it can be entertaining if you are travelling with kids. The basic idea is that the place is filled with 3D "trick" photos. You can then step inside these photos to give the illusion that you are part of the painting, whether that's swimming in an underwater scene or having a waterfall gush down on you.

(Jl. Nakula No.33X, Legian, Kuta; http://dmzbali.com/eng)

31. Marvel at the Hindu Sculptures in Garuda Wisnu Kencana

While Islam is the official religion of Indonesia, you will find that Hinduism is much more prevalent across Bali, and you'll be able to see this first hand in the Garuda Wisnu Kencana park, which is a cultural park, filled with huge Hindu sculptures. The main sculpture is still in ongoing construction, but once finished will be the tallest statue on the island at 145 metres. The brass sculpture will depict Vishnu riding on the back of his Garuda, a mythical Hindu bird.

(Jl. Raya Uluwatu, Ungasan, Kuta Sel; http://gwkbali.com)

32. Get to Grips With Balinese Textiles at Museum Kain

If you have any interest in textiles, Bali is absolutely the place to be, and Museum Kain is the place to really get under the skin of Balinese textiles culture. This museum is especially great at displaying rare batik cloths, a particular type of Balinese handicraft. Even more fascinating, you'll get to learn about the tools and production processes involved in this art form.

(Jl. Pantai Kuta, Kuta)

33. Splash Around at Waterbom Bali

Travelling with kids is both a blessing and a curse. Of course, it's wonderful to give them memories that will last for many years to come, but it's also a major challenge to keep kids entertained day in day out. So if the kids are getting bored of lazy beach days, give them some adventure at the Waterbom Bali waterpark. There are attractions for every age, and even a swim-up bar for when you want to kick back and relax with an ice cold cocktail.

(Jl. Kartika, Tuban, Kuta; www.waterbom-bali.com)

34. Take in the Unique Architecture of Karangasem Royal Palace

The Karangasem Royal Palace can be found on the east part of the island where you will typically find fewer tourists. The palace was created in the 19th century by the first king of the Karangasem kingdom, and it is known for its combination of different architectural styles. The typical Balinese style can be found on the Hindu carvings on the reliefs of the walls, a European style can be seen in the main building and its huge veranda, and the windows and ornaments around the palace are created in the Chinese style.

(Tumbu, Karangasem Sub-District, Karangasem Regency)

35. Eat Like a King and Order Bebek Betutu

When you're on holiday, it's the time when you can forget about the calories for a moment, and have a real taste of decadence. And there is one dish that epitomises culinary indulgence more than any other: Bebek Betutu. Basically this is a whole duck, that is stuffed with all kinds of delicious things, wrapped in banana leaves, and cooked for a long time over coals. It is stuffed with shallots, galangal, garlic, kaffir lime leaves, red chillies, lemongrass, turmeric, nutmeg, spinach, coriander seeds, lime juice, and more.

36. Get Close to the Turtles at Turtle Island Bali

When you've had enough of lazy beach days, one of the fun day trips that you can make in Bali is to Turtle Island. This small island is only accessible by boat, but there are plenty of tour companies that will take you there and back. As the name of the island would suggest, it is a breeding ground for turtles, and the highlight of a trip there is certainly seeing the baby turtles, releasing them into the ocean, and even feeding the turtles. There's also great waves so don't forget your surfboard if that's what you're into.

37. Pay Your Respects at the Bali Bombing Memorial

While Bali is typically a very safe place, there was a very sad occurrence in October of 2002, which left 202 people in Bali dead. A terrorist group were responsible for a bombing in the popular Kuta area, and many locals and tourists were killed as a result. Now there is a permanent memorial site on Legion street that pays respects to the victims of this terrorist attack.

(Jl. Legian Kaja No.38, Kuta)

38. Go Dolphin Watching From Lovina Beach

Dolphins are some of the most magical creatures on planet Earth, and seeing them up close is something that's really quite special. Fortunately, there is a thriving dolphin population off the coast of Bali, and particularly by Lovina Beach, which is a small coastal town at the northern edge of the island. You'll go out into the open water to the places where there is the highest concentration of dolphin pods so that you have a really good chance of getting up close to these gorgeous sea mammals.

39. Learn Something at the Bali Museum in Denpasar

Museum buffs would probably choose a trip to somewhere like New York or Paris over Bali, but if you find yourself on the island on a rainy day and you fancy learning something new, the Bali museum in Denpasar is really a very good choice. Its displays typically have English translations, and you can see artefacts relating to

Balinese architecture, typical dress, households, and ceremonial objects. There's even a few prehistoric pieces, such as stone and bronze tools.

(Jl. Mayor Wisnu No.1, Dangin Puri, Denpasar Tim., Kota Denpasar)

40. Get Decadent on the Double-Six Rooftop

Yes, there is tonnes to see and do and Bali, but sometimes all you want to do is kick back in a beautiful setting with a cocktail in hand, right? Right. And that's why you should know about the Double-Six Rooftop, which is, in our opinion, the very best rooftop bar on the whole of the island. You'll have a spectacular view of one of Bali's most popular beaches, and a huge variety of cocktails to choose from. Don't miss the Pandan Daiquiri.

(Jalan Pantai Double Six No.66, Seminyak, Kuta; www.double-six.com)

41. Shop for Upcycled Treasures at UpCycle in Kuta

Looking for some unique gifts to take home with you from Bali? Look no further than a store that goes by the name of UpCycle in Kuta. If you're not familiar with the idea of upcycling, it basically involves taking something that would be thrown out and updating its style or transforming it into a totally different and cool object. At this store you will find things like old drinking cans and vinyl albums totally transformed into bags, purses, bracelets, picture frames, and more.

(Jl Arjuna, Kuta)

42. Stretch Your Legs on the Campuhan Ridge Walk

If you're the type of traveller who likes to fill their days with lots of outdoor activities, there are plenty of hikes to enjoy around Bali, and we particularly enjoy the Campuhan Ridge Walk just outside of Ubud. You don't need to be a fitness guru to enjoy this hike because it's 2 kilometres and quite easy. As you walk, you will see river valleys and rice fields, and as the hike draws to a close you'll be greeted by a little town with cafes and galleries.

43. Indulge in Skewer After Skewer of Sate Lilit

Indonesia is a country that's jam packed full of delicious eats, and chicken satay is something that you are probably already familiar with. Well, Bali has its own version of satay called Sate Lilit. There are a few differences. First of all, the skewer is always a blade of lemongrass, which imparts its distinctive taste. Secondly, instead of being covered in peanut, it's covered in coconut. The result is something very tropical tasting.

44. Go Out to Sea on a Glass Bottomed Boat

If you are not the kind of person who likes to get into the ocean with activities like snorkelling or scuba diving, but you would still like to get up close to some of the beautiful marine life and coral around the coast of Bali, another option is to take a trip on a boat with a glass bottom. Because there is so much coast in Bali, you can take the trip from many locations, but a popular place with a few of these types of tours is Tanjung Benoa Beach.

45. Watch Pearl Farming in Action at Atlas Pearl Farm

Want to see a different side of Bali away from the sand and surf? Then find your way to Atlas Pearl Farm, which as the name suggests is a working pearl farm that harvests the jewels of the ocean. The staff here are very friendly and are very happy to talk to you about their profession and the process of farming for pearls. They also sell their own pearls, which could just make for really exceptional and unique Balinese gifts.

(Penyabangan, Gerokgak, Buleleng Regency)

46. Tuck Into a Balinese Snack Called Tum Ayam

When it's that kind of 4pm hour when lunch has long gone but dinner isn't nearly close enough, you might be tempted to reach for an unhealthy snack. But while in Bali, you can reach for a local snack called Tum Ayam, which is so much better than any chocolate bar or packet of crisps. Essentially, minced chicken is mixed with coconut milk, shallots, garlic, ginger, chilli, and other spices, wrapped in a banana leaf and then steamed. It's pretty healthy and tastes incredible. We always go back for seconds.

47. Go Horse Riding on Seminyak Beach

It's no secret that Bali has some of the most spectacular beaches to be found anywhere in the world, but if you are not so much of a beach bum, there are alternative ways to enjoy the sand. How about some horse riding on

Seminyak beach, for example? There are actually several stables close to the beach that can take you on a guided ride, and it's no problem if you have never ridden before. Have a simple canter on the beach, or adventure further into the rice paddies.

48. Find Inner Peace at the Bali Silent Retreat

21st century life can be difficult, and most people have to juggle a million different responsibilities at once. Every now and then, it can be a good idea to simply drop out of those responsibilities and find peace within some quiet time. If that sounds good to you then you should definitely consider a stay at the Bali Silent Retreat, a meditation retreat that has simple wooden bungalows, pretty much in the middle of nowhere. It could be just what you are looking for.

(Banjar Mongan,, Penatahan, Penebel; www.balisilentretreat.com)

49. Extend on the White Sand of Gunung Payung

There's one thing that we want from Bali above anything else, and that's plenty of time on the beach, catching some rays and reading a good book. In our opinion, there's a number of really underrated beaches across the island, and one of the underrated beaches of Bali we always try to visit is Gunung Payung. This beach is pretty remote on the south coast, and that's what keeps it untouched. The waters here are also calmer and more swimmable than the popular surf spots.

50. Dance Dance Dance at Ultra Bali

Bali is a part of Southeast Asia that is no stranger to epic beach parties, but if you really want to take your party spirit to the next level, then make sure you coincide your Bali trip with the annual Ultra Bali Festival, which is hosted across a couple of days each September at the Potato Head Beach Club. If electronic music is what does it for you, you'll love this festival, and previous performers have included Afrojack and Marin Garrix.

(https://ultrabali.com)

51. Visit a 10th Century Hindu Temple, Tirta Empul

There is no shortage of impressive Hindu temples to be found around Bali, and one of the most impressive of the bunch dates all the way back to the 10th century and goes by the name of Tirta Empul. This temple is actually more famous for the baths in front of it as this is a place where local Hindus flock to in order to bathe in the holy water. There are guides on the premises that give very informative tours of the temple.

(Jalan Tirta, Manukaya, Tampaksiring)

52. Shop for Incredible Textiles at Threads of Life

During your trip to Bali, you will no doubt want to shop for some souvenirs that will always remind you of this magical island, and probably some gifts for friends and families too. There are lots of handicrafts to be found on the island, and for textiles we would recommend a shop called Threads of Life in Ubud. The shop works with traditional weavers around the island to bring you all kinds of hand dyed textiles, so whether you want a tote bag or a whole new set of curtains, you are sure to find what you are looking for.

(Jl. Kajeng No.24, Ubud, Gianyar, Kabupaten Gianyar; http://threadsoflife.com)

53. Watch the Negara Bull Races

Negara is an inland town, about 3 hour's drive from Kuta, and not many tourists make it there. But if you feel like witnessing something a little out of the ordinary, we'd highly recommend taking a trip there to watch the Negara Bull Races, which take place every Sunday from June to October. Bulls are decorated with colourful accessories, and hitched in pairs to chariots that jockeys that to steer around the course. It can be a lot of fun.

54. Trek to Bali's Highest Point, Mount Agung

If you'd rather get your heartbeat going than sit on the beach all day, one of the most adrenaline inducing activities on the island is a trek up Mount Agung, the highest point of the island, which also happens to be an active volcano. The trek to the top (3000 metres) takes about 6 hours to complete, and so it's important that you have a decent fitness level before you attempt it. And remember, once you get to the top, you also have to get back down, so be sure to set off early in the morning, and preferably with a guide.

55. Discover Balinese Paintings and Woodcarvings at Puri Lukisan Museum

The Puri Lukisan Museum is the oldest museum in the whole island of Bali, and is dedicated to showcasing traditional Balinese paintings and woodcarvings. The variety here is very impressive. In the east building you'll find classical 16th century wayang-style paintings, in the north building there are the dreamiest ink drawings you've ever seen, and the west building is dedicated to the vibrant post-war paintings of local Balinese artists. There's also a bookshop and café on-site.

(Jl. Raya Ubud)

56. Get Decadent at the Pod Chocolate Factory

There are two types of people in this life. People who love nothing more than to chow down to silky smooth chocolate, and people who we just can't begin to understand. If you love chocolate as much as we do, then a trip to the Pod Chocolate Factory is a must while you're visiting Bali. This factory makes chocolates from source on the island, and on your visit you can learn about the process, and even have a go at making chocolate yourself.

Of course, there will be plenty of opportunities to taste the good stuff too.

(Jalan Tukad Ayung, Carangsari, Petang; http://podbali.com)

57. Go White Water Rafting on the Ayung River

Tired of lazy beach days and want to have a real adventure in the gorgeous landscapes of the island? Then you should seriously consider a spot of white water rafting on the Ayung River. The rapids here are of a level 2 and 3, which means that you'll certainly get thrown about a bit, but you shouldn't worry about being a beginner. There are plenty of adventure companies that will take care of the whole experience, provide all the equipment you need, and show you a great time.

58. Speed Down the Abyss Zipline

Did you know that Bali is not one island but is actually a collection of seven? If you want to get off the beaten track, you should definitely explore some of the smaller islands, and we are particularly fond of Nusa Ceningan, which is home to the Abyss Zipline, a must for anyone with an adventurous spirit. This zipline actually connects the cliff faces of Nusa Ceningan and Nusa Lembongan, so you get to ride above the open water.

59. Get Into the Festival Spirit at Bestival Bali

Bestival is a music festival that is known all over the world for its epic party each September on the Isle of Wight in the UK, but did you know that Bestival also has an offering in Bali? If you're a hedonist at heart, you need to be there. It has the same inclusive and fun ethos as the regular Bestival, but it's better because you're on a tropical island – duh! It takes place at the end of September each year, and performers have included Rudimental, The Cuban Brothers, and Alt-J. See ya there.
(www.bestivalbali.com)

60. Get Back to Nature at the Batukaru Farmstay

Bali is a travel destination that has it all, so if you aren't into the whole surfing and beach party theme, there are plenty of opportunities to enjoy a slower pace and get back to nature as well. And our number one spot to let the cares of the world slide from our shoulders is the Batukaru Farmstay, located in a small village on the slopes of

Batukaru. You'll be staying in a hut, you'll be surrounded by coffee plants, and everything you eat will be harvested from the farm or surrounding farms.

(Banjar Anyar, Batukaru)

61. Enjoy a Heaped Plate of Lawar

One dish that is uniquely Balinese is called Lawar, and somehow it manages to combine fresh, fruity, salty, sweet, and savoury flavours all at once. You can think of this as a big mixed salad and the main ingredients are green beans, beaten eggs, kaffir lime leaves, coconut milk, palm sugar, fried shallots, and fresh grated coconut. This is all mixed together with some kind of meat – usually chicken or pork. If you really want to amp up the savoury element, it can also be mixed with the blood of an animal. This dish can be found in warungs all over the island.

62. Be Stunned by an Ancient Temple, Pura Besakih

Pura Besakih is the largest and most important Hindu temple anywhere in Bali, and it's well worth a visit for those who wish to gain an understanding of the cultural side of this beautiful island. Actually, this is more than one temple, and is actually a complex of 23 temples perched on a hillside, the largest of which is built on six levels, terraced up the slope of the hill. More than seventy festivals are hosted at the temples each year, so you stand a good chance of seeing the temple while its brought to life with Hindu celebrations.

(Besakih, Rendang, Karangasem Regency)

63. Discover Village Life at Nusa Lembongan

Considering it's just one island, there is a lot of diversity to be found in Bali. You'll have no trouble getting acquainted with the surf culture, the hippie culture, and the lush greenery, but what about the regular village life of the local population? For that, we'd love to recommend Lembongan, which is a tiny island off the southeast of Bali. You can enjoy a few activities here, but the real joy is kicking back and watching the slow pace of local life in action.

64. Chow Down on a Local Sweet Treat Called Laklak

While sweet treats are certainly popular in Asian countries, they often aren't so good at producing cakes and pastries.

But one cake that you have to try while in Bali is called Laklak. It is native to the island and combines rice flour with maize, coconut milk, sugar, and boiling water. Sometimes pandan leaves are also added, which give an interesting floral note to the cake, and a vivid green colour.

65. Eat and Shop at Sanur Night Market

When it comes to things to do in the evening time, you have many options in Bali, and one of our favourite things is to stroll the aisles of a night market, and explore all of the different local foods, and perhaps pick up some handicrafts as well. Sanur Night Market is one of the best of the bunch. We particularly like this market because of its local feel, and you'll definitely see more Balinese people and fewer tourists here. It's also a great place to visit if you are on a budget because local people means local prices.
(Jl. Ps. Sindu No.5, Sanur)

66. Discover a World of Gold and Silver in Celuk Village

Looking to take back something really special from Bali, or perhaps you want to go the extra mile with gifts for friends and family from this vacation? Then please do try and make it to Celuk Village, which is a century old village that specialises in the craft of gold and silver jewellery. The exquisite work that comes from this village is so respected that it was often the choice of the local royal family and nobleman.

67. Indulge With a Fancy Meal at Bambu Restaurant

We know that Southeast Asia is something of a budget travel destination, but even budget backpackers have to splurge now and again. And if you only have enough budget to eat one fancy meal during your time in Bali, make sure that it's at the Bambu Restaurant in the Seminyak area. The food here is Indonesian with a twist. The slow roasted duck is unforgettable. Remember to dress up and, of course, enjoy.

(Jl. Petitenget No.198, Kerobokan Kelod, Kuta Utara; http://bamburestaurant.business.site)

68. Shop for Custom Made Surf Boards at Luke Studer

It's no secret that Bali is one of the most popular destinations for keen surfers. Of course, you have the opportunity to ride plenty of waves, but even more than that, you can immerse yourself in a complete surfing culture, and while you're there it can be a great idea to stock up on some surfing goodies. At Luke Studer, you can have your very own custom board made for you, and at a fraction of a price that you would pay at home.
(Jl. Dewi Sri, Legian, Kuta; www.studersurfboards.com)

69. Watch the Water Gush Down at Nungnung Waterfall

Fancy immersing yourself in the glorious beauty of Bali without spending money and all while avoiding other tourists? Then simply make your way to Nungnung Waterfall, which is located in a small town of the same name in the Petang area. Getting to the falls isn't that easy because you have to walk down a gorge with around 500 steps (and you'll have to walk back up again!), but you'll be greeted by the most idyllic sight. And better yet, you can actually swim in the pool created by the waterfall, so don't forget your swimsuit.

70. Learn Indonesian at the Cinta Bahasa Language School

Are you planning on staying in Bali for longer than the span of a regular holiday? Then it can be a really fantastic idea to try and learn the local language. Nobody is saying that learning Indonesian is an easy task, but this is not to say it's impossible, and how cool would it be if you could traverse the aisles of a local night market and actually converse with local people in their own language? There are a few language schools dotted around, but the Cinta Bahasa Language School has the best reputation.

(Jl. Raya Sanggingan No. 88, Indomaret 2nd Floor, Kedewatan, Ubud; http://cintabahasa.com)

71. Enjoy the Luxe Hippie Vibe of Karma Beach

Beach time is a priority when you're in Bali, but with so many postcard perfect beaches strewn across the island, it can actually be hard to pick one. For us, there is a beach called Karma Kandara that never disappoints. The sand is powdery and white, and the ocean is clear. But all of the action centres around Karma Beach Bali, a restaurant, bar and club on the beach that has a luxurious yet bohemian vibe at the same time.

(Karma Kandara Bali, Jalan Villa Kandara, Ungasan; https://karmagroup.com/karma-beach)

72. Take in the Festivities of Galungan

If you would like to get to know the spiritual side of Bali, away from beach parties and surf, be sure to investigate Galungan, a holiday celebrated both at the beginning of April and November. This festival celebrates the triumph of Good over Evil, so it's something that absolutely everyone can relate to. You'll know when Galungan is happening because there are huge poles that sprout up all over the island, decorated with coconut leaves, flowers, and fruit. On the day of the festival itself, virtually everyone will be at the local temple to give their offerings

73. Get Close to Wildlife at Bali Safari and Marine Park

Are you the kind of person who loves animals and likes nothing more than to feel connected with nature? You're in luck, because Bali is a paradise, but you can do one better and see all kinds of wildlife in one place at the Bali Safari and Marine Park. This is one of the largest and most visited animal theme parks on the island, with over 60 animal species that roam free in spacious surroundings that mimic their natural habitats. Some of the animal highlights include Himalayan bears, African hippos, and blue wildebeests.

(Jl. Bypass Prof. Dr. Ida Bagus Mantra Km. 19,8, Serongga, Kec. Gianyar; www.balisafarimarinepark.com/home)

74. Dare to Hike Up an Active Volcano

If you love nothing more than to get outside in Mother Nature and really raise your heartbeat, how about a brisk hike up an active volcano? You got it. The Mount Batur sunrise hike is actually one of the most popular hikes on the island, and it's with good reason. You really do need a local guide for this one, because you'll be starting in the very early hours of the morning, in total darkness, so that you can reach the peak to watch the beautiful sunrise. Your muscles will hurt for a few hours, but this is not an unbearable climb, and the view from the top is so worth it.

75. Visit an Ancient Temple in the Jungle, Pura Gunung Lebah

There are quite a few majestic Hindu temples dotted around Bali, and what makes Pura Gunung Lebah stand out from the crowd is that it's totally surrounded by dense jungle and foliage. The setting is really magical, so this ancient temple is worth seeking out. You will find yourself on the edge of a river listening to the water trickling by and the breeze in the leaves, all while taking in the elaborate carvings of the temple.

(Jl. Raya Ubud No.23, Sayan, Ubud)

76. Indulge a Sweet Tooth With Bali's Black Rice Pudding

Do you have something of a sweet tooth? Then we can guarantee that you are going to fall head over heels for the local black rice pudding, which for something sweet is actually pretty healthy, and can be eaten as a dessert, snack, and it's commonly eaten for breakfast too. This is a simple mixture of black rice, coconut milk, and palm sugar, and it is often topped with banana and chia seeds. It's vegan and gluten free to boot.

77. Have a Snorkelling Experience Off Menjangan Island

Anybody who visits the beaches of Bali knows that it's an exceptionally beautiful place, but we think that it's even more beautiful underneath the ocean, which is typically crystal clear and teeming with tropical fish and coral. One of the best spots to have a snorkelling adventure while in Bali is off Menjangan Island. As well as the smaller species of fish, if you're really lucky you might even see some things like turtles, whale sharks, and mantas here.

78. Learn About Indonesia's Ethnic Groups at Taman Nusa

If you are the kind of person who thinks that walking around stuffy museums is totally boring, we think that you might enjoy Taman Nusa, which operates like a museum in that its purpose is to teach you something, but the whole thing is outdoors and interactive. This cultural park showcases the cultures of various ethnic groups that exist around Indonesia through different houses and buildings, crafts, music and dance performances, and more.

(Jl. Taman Bali, Br. Blahpane Kelod, Desa Sidan; www.taman-nusa.com)

79. Take in the Processions of the Pagerwesi Festival

Bali is more than an island of beaches and surfing, but also an island of culture and tradition. One of the local celebrations you won't want to miss is called Pagerwesi. It takes place every 210 days, and its focus is on strengthening the mind against evil spirits and forces. This is a very ancient festival that mostly involves the giving of offerings to the Universe Creator as a means of protection.

80. Enjoy the Veggie Side of Local Cuisine With Urab

To be honest with you, Balinese food is pretty meat heavy. If you are vegetarian or just feel like something without meat, one local dish that you can sample is called Urab, which can be thought of as a Balinese salad. Lots of interesting veggies are used, such as young cassava leaf, papaya leaf, spinach, water spinach, longbeans, cabbage, and beansprouts. This mix is seasoned with tamarind, chilli pepper, galangal, shallots, garlic, salt, and coconut sugar.

81. Enjoy the Quiet Life at Side by Side Organic Farm

If you want to have a totally different accommodation experience while you're in Bali, you might want to consider a stay on the Side by Side Organic Farm, which is located in a remote village in East Bali, away from the main tourist drag. There is the option to stay cheaply on the farm and help out with tasks, giving you a totally different take on Balinese life. Or if you just feel like stopping by, you can eat lunch at the on-site restaurant, which serves food from the farm itself.

(Padang Kerta, Karangasem Sub-District)

82. Explore the Unexplored at the Secret Gardens of Sambungan

Bali is such a well known travel destination that you might expect every inch of it to be overrun with travellers, but this is far from the case. Bali is actually pretty big, and if you head to the north of the island, you will find plenty of space as well as peace and quiet. If you want to find paradise on earth, look no further than the Secret Gardens of Sambungan, a chain of cascading waterfalls and natural pools deep in the jungle. It's not easy to get there, which is why it's unexplored, but if you can manage the 3 hour trek into the depths of the Balinese rainforest, you certainly won't regret it.

83. Get Literary at the Ubud Writers and Readers Festival

Are you a bookworm at heart? The beaches of Bali are a wonderful place to get away from it all and get some great reading done, but if you are super super serious about reading and writing (perhaps you are a writer yourself) you should acquaint yourself with the annual Ubud Writers and Readers Festival. This is the leading literary festival in all of Southeast Asia, with book signings, Q&A sessions with successful authors, panel discussions, workshops, and more. It takes place each year in October.

(www.ubudwritersfestival.com)

84. Go Jet Ski-ing on Tanjung Benoa Beach

If you are more into adventurous activities on the water than lazy beach time, head to Tanjung Benoa Beach, which has a reputation of being the beach for people with an adventurous spirit. One of the most popular activities there is jet ski-ing. The schools on the beach can cater for total beginners and provide everything that you need, so all you need to do is feel the ocean breeze in your hair as you speed across the water.

85. Get Down to Smooth Sounds at the Ubud Village Jazz Festival

Jazz music is not, of course, a product of Balinese culture. It emerged from the south of the United States in the twentieth century – but this is not to say that you cannot enjoy some smooth jazz sounds while you are visiting Bali, and if you are a jazz lover through and through you need to know about the annual Ubud Village Jazz Festival. It takes place in August each year and attracts jazz talent from across Indonesia, and indeed the globe.

86. Try the Indonesian Version of Meatballs, Bakso

Meatballs is one of those comfort food dishes that absolutely everybody loves, and if you find yourself craving meatballs while in Bali, you'll be pleased to know that there is actually a Balinese version called Bakso. The meatball itself is made from a beef paste, and is springier and softer than a Western meatball. It is typically served in a big bowl of broth with rice noodles and wontons, but you can find other versions that include tofu, hard boiled egg, and more.

87. Ride an Underwater Scooter Across the Ocean

On an island like Bali, you would expect there to be lots of things you can do in the water, from snorkelling to surfing, but have you ever heard of riding an underwater scooter across the bed of the ocean? Nor had we until we ventured to Bali. Admittedly the scooter moves pretty slowly, but you wouldn't want it to zoom across the ocean floor when there is so much to look at. You are fitted into your own helmet with oxygen and there is no need for a tank.

(www.baliunderwaterscooter.com)

88. Experience the Thrill of Kitesurfing in Sanur

If you are a true adventurer at heart, you should definitely have a go at kitesurfing at least once, and Bali is the perfect place for trying this extreme sport. So you are stood on a board about the size of a wakeboard, and you hold a kite in the air, which powers your movements, giving and extra thrill to the surfing experience. Sanur beach is a popular place to try this out with schools that can rent equipment and provide kitesurfing lessons.

89. Relax in a Natural Infinity Pool, Angel's Billabong

Bali isn't just one island but a series of seven, so if you want to get a little bit off the beaten track, there is plenty of opportunity to visit the smaller, lesser known islands. On an island that goes by the name of Nusa Penida you can find something extra special – a natural infinity pool called Angel's Billabong. The water is a gorgeous emerald green colour, and it's the perfect place for a swim in a picturesque place with nothing but peace and quiet around you.

90. Discover Local Art at Rudana Gallery

If you are an artsy kind of person, it's well worth seeking out the Rudana Museum, which is dedicated to showcasing modern and post-modern Indonesian art. The gallery has a permanent exhibition but also temporary exhibitions so you will get to see something new every time that you visit. You might even get to see come local contemporary artists working on-site.

(JL. Peliatan, Ubud)

91. Unwind in the Tabanan Hot Springs

There is nothing quite as relaxing as soaking your cares away in some gorgeous natural hot springs. There are actually a few of these dotted around Bali, but our pick of the bunch are the Tabanan Hot Springs. What we love the most about these natural hot springs is the view you have all around you of beautifully green rice paddies. We can think of nothing better to induce a state of total relaxation.

92. Soak up Some Rays on Balangan Beach

When you're visiting Bali, it's a given that you will want to soak up a few rays on the beach. But actually, there are so many beaches dotted around the island that it can be hard to know which one to go for. If you have a limited amount of time, we'd definitely recommend seeking out Balangan Beach. It's only 15 minutes or so out of busy Kuta, but the whole feel of the place is 100% different. This small strip of white sand exists below rocky cliffs, and it's the perfect place to have some quiet beach time or hit the waves without jostling against other surfers

93. Eat Fresh Seafood by the Ocean at the Echo Beach Club

Whenever we visit an island, we think of it as our duty to eat as much fresh seafood as humanly possible, and while there are plenty of great seafood options in Bali, our favourite spot of the bunch would have to be the Echo Beach Club. Whether you want a seafood kebab, seared scallops, or all the deliciousness of a whole lobster, the choice is yours. It's also situated directly on the beach with a killer view.

(Jalan Pura Batu Mejan, Canggu, Kuta Utara; www.echobeachhouse.com)

94. Buy Food at Rock Bottom Prices at Taman Sari Market

The Taman Sari Market is not the kind of market that is built with tourists in mind. It is a hive of conflicting smells, sights, and tastes, and in our opinion it's all the better for it. Because this is the place where locals buy their produce, you will be able to find incredible food at rock bottom prices. The market is open all day. Go in the morning if you want to pick up things like fresh fruit, and the in the evening you can expect more of a night market feel with freshly grilled chicken satay and noodle soups.
(Jl. Tangkuban Perahu No.1, Kerobokan Kelod, Kuta Utara)

95. Find the Giant Banyan Tree in Gesing

In a small town that goes by the name of Gesing, it's possible to locate an absolutely massive Banyan tree that has a height of 85 metres, and is thought to be over 700 years old. These trees are particularly statuesque and have incredible winding aerial roots. But more than this, these trees are very special to the Balinese because they are thought to possess spirits and demons. Legend has it that if you pray to the tree, it will grant your wishes.

96. Discover the Wayang Art of Kamasan Village

If you want to discover the local arts scene in Bali, it's true that there's a tonne of galleries that you can explore, but we would really recommend paying a visit to Kamasan Village if you would like to have more of a local experience. This is where you can see local Balinese people creating traditional Wayang paintings, the likes of which would be much more expensive when sold through a gallery. It's also a wonderful place to find gold and silver objects.

97. Become a Flexible Yogi

One of the most popular activities for holiday-makers in Bali is to stretch their limbs and enjoy a few sessions of yoga. Whether you are intrigued by the idea of taking a yoga class for the first time, or you want to treat yourself to an immersive yoga retreat, Bali is the place where you can find everything to meet your yoga needs, and it won't matter which part of the island you are staying on. You might just leave as a professional yogi.

98. Start the Day With a Bowl of Bubur Mengguh in Buleleng

As the saying goes, breakfast is the most important meal of the day, and this is never truer than when you are travelling from place to place and need all the energy that you can muster. A typical Balinese breakfast dish that hails from the town of Buleleng is called Bubur Mengguh. If you've ever tried congee before, it can be thought of as comparable to this. This is a savoury porridge made with rice and coconut milk, and delicious slices of chicken and local vegetables.

99. Visit the Largest Bamboo Structure in the World

Bamboo is a commodity that is very prevalent across Bali, and fortunately all of this bamboo is put to good use in the local architecture. In fact, the largest bamboo structure in the whole world can be found on the island. Big Tree Farm is actually a chocolate factory, and lies just half an hour outside of Ubud. You are welcome to tour the factory, and learn about different types of cacao and the process of creating delicious chocolate.

(Piakan, Sibangkaja, Abiansemal, Sibang Kaj;
http://bigtreefarms.com)

100. Party With Hipsters at the Sunny Side Up Festival

We think that there is nothing quite as fun as a summer festival, and the annual Sunny Side Up Festival in Bali is the type of festival that has something for absolutely everyone. Of course, it attracts world class music performers and DJs, but it also has a cultural side with cutting edge artists showcasing visual works, dance performances, and more. Some of the artists that have performed at the festival include Mark Ronson, Ellie Goulding, Jessie Ware, and Disclosure. It takes place each August at the Potato Head Beach Club.
(www.sunnysideupfest.com)

101. Explore the Goa Gala-Gala Underground House

Something really off the beaten track that is wonderful to explore when you've had enough surf and sand is the Goa Gala-Gala Underground House on the island of Nusa Lembongan (which is also a part of Bali, FYI). This underground house was inspired by the designs of the Mahabharata, and is a full underground world, complete with a kitchen, dining room, living room, hallways and bedrooms. Because the house is underground, it's well protected from the heat and humidity of the island.

Before You Go...

Thanks for reading **101 Amazing Things to Do in Bali.**
We hope that it makes your trip a memorable one!

Have a great trip!

Team 101 Amazing Things

Made in the USA
Lexington, KY
07 July 2019